THE MARTYR OF ALLAHABAD

THE MARTYR OF ALLAHABAD

MEMORIALS OF ENSIGN ARTHUR MARCUS HILL CHEEK, OF THE SIXTH NATIVE BENGAL INFANTRY, MURDERED BY THE SEPOYS AT ALLAHABAD

ROBERT MEEK

GYAN

Published by

Gyan Publishing House
5, Ansari Road
Daryaganj, New Delhi-110002
Phone: 011-47034999, 9811692060
E-mail: books@gyanbooks.com

Distribution Network
gyanbooks.com
India, USA, Canada, UK, Australia

ISBN: 978-93-7447-275-0 (PB)

First Published, 1858

2nd Impression 2026

Printed at: Gyan Press, Delhi.

THE MARTYR OF ALLAHABAD
Author: ROBERT MEEK

Your loving son

Marcus.

THE MARTYR OF ALLAHABAD.

MEMORIALS

OF

ENSIGN ARTHUR MARCUS HILL CHEEK,

OF THE

Sixth Native Bengal Infantry,

MURDERED BY THE SEPOYS AT ALLAHABAD.

BY

THE REV. ROBERT MEEK, M.A.,
RECTOR OF SUTTON BONNINGTON, NOTTS;
AUTHOR OF "THE MUTUAL RECOGNITION OF GLORIFIED SAINTS,"
"HEAVENLY THINGS," ETC., ETC.

The Fifth Thousand, with Additions.

LONDON:
JAMES NISBET AND CO., 21, BERNERS-STREET.
1858.

TO

THE RIGHT HONOURABLE

THE LORD ARTHUR MARCUS CECIL HILL, K.T.S.,

These Memorials

OF

HIS GODSON, ARTHUR MARCUS HILL CHEEK,

(WITH HIS LORDSHIP'S PERMISSION,)

ARE RESPECTFULLY DEDICATED

BY

THE AUTHOR.

SUTTON RECTORY,
LOUGHBOROUGH, NOTTS.

CONTENTS.

CHAPTER I.

EARLY DAYS.—DEPARTURE FOR INDIA.—JOINS THE REGIMENT, ETC.

THE year 1857 will be long remembered as a time of sore trouble, and of deep and wide-spread affliction, from the fearful outbreaks of mutiny and violence in India. The progress of these mutinies among the native soldiery has from the beginning been marked by fearful massacres and atrocities, unparalleled in the history of ancient or modern times. The accounts of the massacres of British officers, of the dishonour and cruelty inflicted on their wives and children, have stirred up a deep feeling of sympathy and of just indignation throughout the nation. Numerous are the families who mourn the loss of beloved friends and relatives thus cruelly cut off by the treacherous mutineers. How many once happy wives have been made widows,—children made orphans,—and parents bereaved of beloved children! Yet, amidst these appalling, heart-rending calamities, there have been exhibited many shining examples of British heroism, of devotion, and piety, the remembrance of which deserves to be recorded for the encouragement and instruction of survivors and posterity.

The design of the following narrative is to supply some particulars of the short life, sufferings, and noble and Christian death of *Arthur Marcus Hill Cheek*, a young ensign of the 6th Bengal Infantry, who, under the age of seventeen years, when enduring cruel sufferings from Mohammedans, exhibited that Christian fidelity and heroism which justly entitle him to the glorious distinction of *the young Christian martyr of Allahabad.* The first notice of this noble boy appeared in the "Times" newspaper, in an extract from a letter of a British officer in India:—

"When the wretched 6th Regiment mutinied at Allahabad, and murdered their officers, an ensign only sixteen years of age, who was left for dead among the rest, escaped in the darkness to a neighbouring ravine. Here he found a stream, the waters of which sustained his life for four days and nights. Although desperately wounded, he contrived to raise himself into a tree during the night for protection from wild beasts. Poor boy! he had a high commission to fulfil, before death released him from his sufferings. On the fifth day he was discovered, and dragged by the brutal sepoys before one of their leaders, to have the little life left in him extinguished. There he found another prisoner, a Christian catechist, formerly a Mohammedan, whom the Sepoys were endeavouring to torment and terrify into a recantation. The firmness of the native was giving way, as he knelt amidst his persecutors, with no human sympathy to support him. The boy officer, after anxiously watching him for a short time, cried out, '*Oh, my friend, come what may, do not deny the Lord Jesus Christ!*' Just at this moment, the alarm of a sudden attack by the gallant Colonel Neile, with his Madras Fusiliers, caused the flight of the murderous fanatics. The catechist's life was saved. He turned to bless the boy whose faith had strengthened his faltering spirit, but the young martyr had passed beyond all reach of human cruelty—he had entered into his rest!"

Thousands in whose hearts this touching, though, in some respects, imperfect story, has awakened admiration, and gratitude to God who strengthened the faith of this gallant youth boldly, in the hour of suffering and death, to confess and glorify Christ, will be interested to receive further particulars respecting him. An opportunity the writer has lately had of converse with the bereaved parents, and the sight of letters received by them from India, and other quarters, will enable him to supply many additional and interesting details.

Arthur Marcus Hill Cheek, the second son of Oswald Cheek, Esq., the highly-respected town clerk of Evesham, was born at Evesham, July 31, 1840. He was the godson of the Right Hon. Lord Arthur Marcus Cecil Hill, formerly M.P. for Evesham, who attended as sponsor at his baptism, and after whom he bore the name of *Arthur Marcus Hill*. His great-grandfather was Nicholas Mosley Cheek, formerly Rector of Rollestone, Staffordshire, and afterwards founder and first minister of St. Stephen's Church, Salford, Manchester, and nephew to the late Sir John Parker Mosley, Bart., of Rollestone. His grandfather is John Mosley Gilbert Cheek, in his 85th year, formerly an eminent solicitor at Evesham, but who for many years has retired from the profession. Our young Christian hero, *Marcus*, for so he was generally called, was one of a large family, nine of whom, with the afflicted parents, live to mourn his early death. There is but little to record of his early days. His parents speak of him as an affectionate and dutiful son, as remarkably steady and correct in conduct, having and manifesting at all times a conscientious regard to truth; as most attentive to his religious duties, fond of attending the services of the Church, and serious in his attention when in the house of God, and careful to keep the Sabbath-day holy. He first went to a school, as a child, near Birmingham, kept by a lady; then removed to the Proprietary School at Edgbaston, near Birmingham; thence he went to the Grammar School at Cheltenham, under the care of Dr. Humphries, who speaks of him as a youth of great promise. Here he received several valuable prizes for good conduct and improvement in his studies.

The following extract from a letter from Dr. Humphrys will be read with interest:—

"*March* 11, 1858.

"He," Marcus Cheek, "came to reside with me as

a boarder in August, 1852. As I have formerly observed, during the first year he exhibited at times an obstinacy of temper which gave me considerable trouble. He was not then under my own teaching. Having carefully watched the course things were taking, I adopted the resolution of having Cheek privately in my study, and making an appeal to his higher and better feelings. This had not the desired effect at first; but after a few such interviews, when he came to understand that I was really acting from kind feelings and with a good motive towards him, the hardness began to give way, and in the course of a few weeks he became, I was thankful to observe, a changed boy, in reference to this one great defect of his character. Sometimes symptoms of the old infirmity would make their appearance, as he acknowledged to me in private, but he struggled manfully, and, I believe, prayerfully, against them; and not without success. Thenceforth, indeed, 'obstinacy' was restrained *within the just and really beneficial limits of firmness and perseverance*. He was not a boy of very bright natural parts, but he maintained a respectable position in his classes, and in some branches of learning for which he had a more decided taste, such as drawing, history, geography, he obtained prizes at our examinations, &c.

"From first to last I ever found Marcus Cheek a *truthful, honourable* boy. When during the first year he occasionally fell into disgrace, with other masters or myself, he would always confess the truth so far as concerned himself; and in any of those little affairs in which boys at school will combine for the commission of some breach of discipline, he was equally firm in declining to betray his comrades. It is no slight praise to be able to say of a pupil that he was eminently *truthful*, *courageous*, *gentlemanly*; and with this there was united, in the latter part of his sojourn with me, a respect for religion and an attention to its duties which promises well, under God's blessing, for the future.

"His conduct gave me every satisfaction to the end. He called here to bid me farewell on his way to India, and deeply have I since regretted that I was not at home at the time.

"I have been confirmed in one opinion—which I have sometimes had hard work to defend—by the history of this lad while under my care; namely, how important it is, and how much the duty of every man who takes upon himself the solemn duties of a school, and especially of a boarding school, to endeavour to get at the heart and feelings of every pupil. I say '*every*,' for I believe that there is some road to every young heart, if we can only find it out; and that can only be done by the gracious help of God.

"I am, dear Sir,

"Yours truly,

"E. R. HUMPHRYS."*

* The pupils of the Cheltenham Grammar School have formed a Committee to raise subscriptions for a *Tablet* to

While resident in Cheltenham, it was the privilege of Marcus Cheek to pass many of his leisure hours with an agreeable family there, by whom he was highly esteemed. In this family were several youths of about his own age, to whom he was greatly attached. The mother of this family, in a letter lately received from her, thus testifies of Marcus :—

"*March* 9, 1858.

"I have but little to write that will bear much on the religious and moral character of dear Marcus Cheek; but the germ of much that was very good was visible constantly in his character. The few letters I enclose, and the trifling incidents I notice, will, I think, be interesting to you, and show you he possessed kind and generous feelings, much observation, a strong predilection for what was right and noble in character, and a desire in his own actions to accord with what he admired in others. I was introduced to him the Midsummer before he went to Brussels, and at a time of relaxation, cheerfulness, and bustle. My eldest son had just returned from his first voyage. Marcus Cheek and some other youths of the same age often met here. All of them were high-spirited, and all eagerly speculating on what might betide them, as all were entering on their several courses for life. In all their discussions

the memory of Marcus Cheek, "*the Martyr of Allahabad,*" to be placed in the school. Subscriptions for this interesting object are received by R. B. Smith, Esq., Honorary Secretary at *the Grammar School, Cheltenham.*

I noticed Marcus Cheek ever paid the most attention to what people far older than himself said, and often, after arguing a point with them, acquiesced in their opinion. His remarks were very pleasant, frank, and open. He had a chivalrous feeling of honour and integrity, quite remarkable in such a youth. He had a great reverence for the Sabbath. One Saturday night (he and his companions had been a long expedition) some of them said they should have a long rest on Sunday morning. I remonstrated a little, and he said, 'That is right, Mrs. E. I shall be up and ready to go to church with you.' He was up and went; and he told me he made a point of going to church; that one of his sisters had convinced him of the good of constantly attending to this his duty, and said she is very constant in visiting the poor and sick. His disposition was remarkably cheerful. He was always happy and merry; very fond of his friends. He was very fond of poetry, and often read pieces from Sir Walter Scott's poems. I asked him one day if he fancied himself one of the heroes. He said, 'You know I may soon be enacting some such scenes; at least sharing in some such exploits.' The time drew near when they had to part. He went to Brussels. The rest soon followed—some to India, some to Australia, &c. They never all met again; but we saw Marcus Cheek the next summer, and he was greatly improved. We afterwards saw him in London, when I heard again of his great amiability of disposition. He dined with us about three months to-day before he met his death.

"A lady called only the day before yesterday, who, on seeing the likeness of him given in your book, said, 'Oh, I have seen him very often when he was at the Grammar School. I sat near him at church, and noticed the earnestness and attention of his behaviour, ever the same.' I have read your truly delightful little book with intense interest and pleasure. I knew he was a gallant, fine youth, but little dreamed of the trials that awaited him, or of the noble death he was so soon to die."

This lady gives an extract from her son's letter—one of the youths before mentioned—of the age of fourteen, to whom she had sent a Worcester paper, announcing the death of Marcus Cheek, and which reached him on his arrival at Calcutta. He writes,—

"I was standing on the gangway one evening, when a coolie came alongside with a paper directed to me. I knew your dear handwriting, and opened it where I stood. The first words I clapped my eyes on was the death of Marcus Cheek. I never was so horrified in my life. I burst into tears where I was standing; I could not help it. I immediately got leave to go below; there I read the account of the massacre. I was confounded. Only think, almost the last evening he spent in England was with us! When I was in my hammock I cried to think of poor Marcus and his noble death!" The mother adds—"Such was my boy's feeling on what he saw in the paper; when he sees your book, and reads what so many good persons have felt on hearing of his noble conduct and martyr-death, I trust a blessing will follow."

Marcus Cheek, after leaving Cheltenham, went to Brussels, where he studied for a year under the care of the Rev. E. J. Jenkins, a British Chaplain in that city. The mother of this gentleman, in a letter of condolence addressed to the parents, thus testifies of Marcus, while under their care:—

"It was with overwhelming sorrow I read his name in the 'Times' yesterday. I cannot resist expressing to you the sincere sympathy I feel for that heavy loss his family have sustained by the death of so promising a youth. Of his good qualities I could give many proofs, but I will not harrow up your feelings, already too sorely tried, and only add, that poor Marcus was a favourite with us all, and deeply his early death is lamented by my son, myself, and his late schoolfellows."

The following extract of a letter to his father, from Brussels, is interesting. In the haste of leaving home Marcus had neglected to pay a small boyish debt he had contracted. His fond father, anxious to impress on the minds of his children a scrupulous regard to honesty and the avoidance of thoughtless expenditure, had kindly remonstrated with him. This will explain the allusion in the following extract:—

"My dear Father,—I am extremely sorry to hear that Mamma is unwell, but I hope her visit to Bretforton will do her good. As yet, my dear father, I have never owed more than two or three shillings, which I forgot to pay Mr. H., for fishing tackle, before I left, and which I had intended to pay, but quite forgot: and the other day, having no money to pay for some letters, one of the boys kindly lent me some until I had some chance of paying him. Thus you have the extent of my debts. I can assure you that I have felt very uncomfortable since I posted the letter, thinking that I owed a few francs. I think I can safely promise never to get into debt, and, at least, this I can safely say, that I detest debt as much as you possibly can. I think it is the root of immense evil, and all manner of temptation; and regarding it in this light I will shun it through life as my worst enemy. God only knows how I can resist the temptation of various vices when I am left to act for myself,—but it shall be my earnest prayer to be delivered from them."

The principles and feelings avowed in this letter of a boy of sixteen are too important to our young readers to be overlooked. It should ever be borne in mind that *honesty* is an essential branch of the religion of Christ, which requires us to "live *righteously* and godly in the present world." How many young men would have been spared difficulties which crippled their exertions in after-life, had they commenced their career with the same honest principles which are expressed by the youthful writer of this letter. It is a lamentable fact that many young people seem to have no idea of the sin and disgrace of contracting debt by thoughtless expenditure. This habit is especially to be avoided in boyhood as the forerunner of many evils. The resolute self-denial of our young hero was but the first demonstration of that firmness of character and conscientiousness which afterwards enabled him to resist the solicitations of those who tempted him to save his life by renouncing his religion.

The fear expressed by this youth as to his endurance and triumph over temptations to evil is also worthy of notice. In the gay capital of Brussels, removed from the watchful eye of parents, he felt his exposure to danger on this score. It was indicative of true religious principles germinating in his mind that he *felt* this, and was distrustful of himself. Such feelings are among the best pledges of safety, as they will lead the young Christian to shun the scenes and occasions of temptations; to watch against the danger, and to pray earnestly to God for upholding and preserving grace. It is to the want of such holy fear, and distrust of themselves, and neglect of prayer, that many young persons, in an unsuspecting hour, fall a prey to temptations which have proved to them the commencement of a career of folly and misery. The religious principles here avowed by young Marcus, sown in the youthful mind and nurtured there, are the elements of true greatness of character, and will be the source of pure joys in after-life.

Before he left Brussels, Marcus, at his own desire, was *confirmed*, and the first Sunday after his return to England, when the Sacrament was to be administered at the church of his native town, he expressed his desire and intention to his mother to partake of the Holy Communion with her, which he did with great seriousness and devotion. About this time, on an occasion of a collection being made in the church, his aunt supposing that he had but little money with him, offered to give him a part of what she intended for the collection, to put in the plate. His reply was, "Oh no, aunt, you know that would not be *my* gift, but *yours*. I intend to give *my own*, and have something to give." Marcus at this time was fond of drawing, and several of his sketches, which the writer has seen in his little room, and which remain as he left them, evince considerable talent in this way; one or two show considerable wit and humour. He was remarkably tall; at the age of fifteen, his stature was within an inch of six feet. Discovering a decided predilection for the military profession, his father, through the kind interest of Lord Marcus Hill, who was attached to him as his godson, obtained an appointment for him, through the Right Hon. Robert Vernon Smith, President of the Board of Control, who gave him a "*direct*" appointment to India. Though such an appointment rendered his going through the usual course of studies for two years at Addiscombe unnecessary, he had to pass an examination there, which he did with credit to himself and satisfaction to those who examined him.

The time was now come for Marcus to quit the scenes of his early youth, and to leave those beloved friends and that home which he was not again to revisit. He was cheerful in spirit, buoyant in hope of future scenes and days, though at times a little depressed, as the time drew nigh of separation from those he loved. His father accompanied him to Southampton, where he embarked for India on the 20th of March, 1857, reaching Calcutta by the overland route on the 28th of April, and received his appointment of ensign of the 6th Regiment of Bengal Infantry, stationed at Allahabad. He was allowed three weeks to visit his uncle and family resident in India before he joined his regiment. The short letters from himself, and others from his relatives, show that these hasty visits were to them all a source of great pleasure and satisfaction. Alas, these were the only, the last visits our young ensign was permitted to make to his Indian relatives! Little did they imagine they should see his face no more. Such was the will of God, and they bow, though with sorrowing hearts and sweet reminiscences of the departed youth, to Him, who "doeth all things well." Young Marcus reached Allahabad on the 19th of May, 1857, and joined his regiment. The brief communications received by his friends in England speak of his being pleased with Allahabad as a fine city, and of the satisfaction he realized in his new position, and the novel circumstances in which he found himself. It is much to be regretted that a diary, which he promised to keep and send monthly to his mother, has not been found, as it would have conveyed interesting information concerning him; this diary, his sword, the Bible given to him by his aged grandfather before he quitted England, and other valuables, are supposed to have been irrecoverably lost.

This brief notice of the early days of *Marcus Cheek*,—though presenting nothing remarkable above that of many young people, yet viewed in connexion with his future short history, furnishes one among many instances that times of great trouble call forth from their obscurity persons of eminent talent and faith who would have remained unknown had all things gone on quietly and smoothly as usual; just as the earthquake and the torrent, rending the mountain side, reveal to sight the rich minerals before concealed. Where there is nothing more than what is commonly expected to take place in the ordinary affairs of life, the man of high courage has no opportunity of distinguishing himself from his timid and irresolute companions. He may not himself even be aware that he possesses those higher virtues that are commonly called forth by difficult and dangerous circumstances. The latent virtue existed before the trial came; it would be too late to learn how to do the duty when the time of action arrived. The great task of those who educate the rising generation must be to implant those high principles of Christian faith, of justice, mercy, and truth, which will render it difficult, if not impossible, for a man to do an act of criminality, of injustice and cruelty, or to violate the strictest rules of honesty and truth. The parent and guardian must strive, in dependance on Divine guidance, to awaken the latent powers of mind, and to kindle high and holy feelings; but there is no teaching more powerful than *example.* The anxious parent, therefore, who sends forth an inexperienced and darling son to encounter the temptations and difficulties of the world, will look with eagerness for some shining examples of virtue among the comrades of the boy, or those of similar age, that may hold forth to him a pattern by which to form his own conduct. Hence, it is important that every deed of heroism, every shining example of piety, should be remembered, that those who hear of it may be stimulated and encouraged to do likewise. Surrounded as the inexperienced youth is with the many bad examples whose influence is to draw to evil, it is refreshing to find some who, though young, have been strong in faith, and have held fast their Christian hope in the darkest hour of temptation and peril. It is, therefore, a sacred duty to preserve the records of the faithful who have stood out bravely to confess Christ before men. In thus gathering up the few precious memorials of Marcus Cheek, as we proceed, we hope to hold up a shining example of Christian fidelity, to stimulate other young persons to cultivate by prayer and diligence those Christian graces which can arm the unprotected sufferer with the same courage to bear affliction, even captivity and torture, without giving up their trust in the power and love of their Saviour.

CHAPTER II.

THE MUTINY AT ALLAHABAD.

The fearful storm, of the near approach of which there were unmistakeable signs,—was now about to burst over Allahabad, its 100,000 inhabitants, and its devoted garrison. What had occurred at Meerut, Neemuch, Benares, and other places,—the fearful massacre of British officers and Europeans,—the flight of the mutineers to Delhi, and its possession by them, with all its mighty stores of military materials, could not fail to excite alarm at Allahabad. It was manifest to all that the mutiny was not, as at first supposed, of a partial or local character, but the result of a deep-laid, well-ordered, and widely-spread conspiracy for the overthrow of British dominion —for the expulsion of Christians and Christianity from India. A time was fixed for striking the final blow, and for a general rising and massacre of the Europeans. The somewhat premature outbreak at Meerut anticipated this—led to the discovery of the fearful plot, and thus providentially put the Europeans on their guard. In Allahabad, with about 100,000 inhabitants, with a large Sepoy force, and with comparatively small

European forces, in the event of an outbreak, the worst of consequences were apprehended. The Rev. Mr. Hay, an American missionary, stationed there and in the city at the time, states:—"There had been several panics in the city for some time before the revolt broke out there, and three weeks before there was any fighting the city was patrolled, and European women and children were ordered into the Fort. At times the alarm died away, and the women would come out of the Fort. The expectation was that the city would be attacked by mutineers from Benares. At length a chief raised the standard of insurrection. No European knew who he was; some said he was a Moulvie—that is, a Mohammedan religious teacher, something like the padre of the Portuguese; others, that he was a native officer; others, that he was a weaver by trade. He, however, represented himself as a Viceroy of the King of Delhi. He commanded about 4,000 of the mutineers. Mr. Hay speaks in the highest terms of Major Brasier and Colonel Neile. He (Brasier) commanded the Sikhs at Allahabad, and exercised great influence over them. It was to him that the Europeans were indebted for preventing the rebels from taking the fort. Had they done so, scarcely anything could have driven them out of it, for it is constructed on a European model. Nothing could induce the rebel Sepoys who besieged it to come near, so much did they dread its guns. On the 13th June, Colonel Neile cannonaded Darghung, a suburb of Allahabad. Brasier behaved there with distinguished gallantry. The chief of the mutineers was taken prisoner. He was a young man magnificently dressed, and was said to be a nephew of the Moulvie who headed the mutiny inside the walls. Major Brasier, surrounded by a few Sikh soldiers, ordered the chief to be brought before him to be interrogated. After being questioned, he was ordered to be taken to a place of confinement. His arms were loosely fastened behind him. Before he left the presence of the Major, he by a great effort caught at a sword that was within his reach, and made a cut at one of the Sikhs. Brasier and all the Sikhs fell upon him, and the former wrested the sword from the prisoner's hand; but the enraged Sikhs, while the chief was prostrate, placed their heels on his head and literally crushed out his brains, and the body was thrown outside the gates there."

Within the city all was intense anxiety and alarm. The 6th Native Regiment of Bengal Infantry, of which Marcus Cheek was an ensign, was for a time considered to be faithful and to be relied on. They had, with great apparent sincerity, professed their loyalty, and great attachment to their officers, and had prayed to be led to Delhi, to rescue that city from the rebels; and had received with hearty cheers the thanks of the Governor-General for their loyalty. But in the hour of need the 6th Regiment proved treacherous and broke out into open mutiny, and massacred their officers, to whom they had professed submission and attachment! The sad story of all this is best told in the extracts from letters of several of the survivors.

FROM A CIVIL SERVANT.

"*Allahabad, June* 28.

"I told you in my last letter that we were apprehensive of an outbreak on the part of the city people, and that I had taken up a position at the gaol, ready to make a stand—that the officers of the 6th Native Infantry had all confidence in their men, though we had not, for now no one can trust those wretched natives. Well, matters went on quietly enough till Friday the 5th, when news of the disturbance at Benares came up, with a report that a number of the insurgents were on their way to attack this station. On the same day an order came from the Brigadier at Cawnpore to 'man the Fort with every available European, and make a good stand.' We non-military men were instantly ordered into the Fort, being formed into a militia under the orders of the officer commanding the garrison. We slept in the Fort on that Friday, the 5th, doing duty upon the ramparts, and returned to the station the following morning, but only for the morning, going into the Fort again in the afternoon. About this time we had in the Fort about fifty invalid artillery soldiers, some few commissariat and magazine sergeants, and we volunteers, mustering above 100 men. There were also 400 Sikhs, and 80 of the wretched 6th guarding the main gate. A great number of the European merchants and half-castes remained outside, believing the report to be only a cry of '*Wolf,*' and supposing it to be a false alarm. The report of the approach of the insurgents was false; but, alas! would that the poor creatures had taken advice, and joined us in the Fort! Among those outside were poor Captain Birch, the Fort-Adjutant, a married man, poor fellow! with a family; Innes, the Executive Engineer, who had the previous day resigned his appointment in the Fort from ill-health, and had gone up to his bungalow. My poor dear friend, Alexander, of the Irregulars, was in a garden near the Fort with 150 of his troopers. Two guns, under Harward, of the Artillery, had been sent down to the river to guard the bridge of boats over the Ganges towards Benares. Hinks, of the 6th Native Infantry, and two little griffs (young men not long in India), were also stationed there, in charge of two companies of that regiment. Well, all these poor fellows were out, and we were inside the Fort, through the mercy of the Almighty. We were told off on our guard, and had laid ourselves down on our beds (those who were not on watch), when about half-past nine we heard firing in the station, and on the alarm-bugle being sounded we ran up to the ramparts in breathless silence. The firing grew heavier, and we all thought that the insurgents had entered the station, and were being beaten off by the regiment. So steady was the musketry, regular the firing; on, on it continued, volley after volley. 'Oh!' we all said, 'those gallant Sepoys are beating off the rebels,'—for the firing grew fainter in the distance, as if they were driving a force out of the station. But before long the sad truth was known. Harward rode in, bringing the tidings that the wretched Sepoys had risen, had seized his guns, and had marched them up to the station. He had escaped, and had run up to poor Alexander's camp, who jumped on his horse and rode up towards the lines, with as many of his men as could be got ready; he had been caught in an ambush by a body of Sepoys lying in wait in an empty tank, and had been killed by a musket being placed to his side, blowing out his heart. His poor body was brought in later in the night, and I gave his hand a last shake and shed tears over his last bed.

"The officers were at mess when the wretches sounded the alarm-bugle to bring them to the parade, and shot them down right and left. Wretched murderers, may they receive their reward! Nine poor little ensigns doing duty with the regiment were bayoneted to death in the mess-room, and three of the officers who escaped heard their cries as they passed! Poor boys! who had never given offence to any native, nor caused dissatisfaction to the Sepoys. Five officers were shot belonging to the regiment, besides the nine poor boys. Birch and Innes, with the Sergeant-Major—in all, seventeen military men,—many merchants and others, were most cruelly murdered. In all, fifty Europeans fell that night by the hands of the murderous Sepoys. The treasury was plundered, the prisoners escaped from gaol, and the work of destruction commenced. The whole station was destroyed—house after house plundered and destroyed! Each moment we expected the Sikhs would turn on us, and then! . . . . But the

Almighty mercifully decreed otherwise. We disarmed the 6th guard at the main gate, and found the villains with loaded and capped muskets ready to turn out!

"What an escape we had! Five officers came in, all having escaped in a wonderful manner—three naked, having had to swim the Ganges. We were all night under arms, and in the morning lay down in our cots sad and weary, each moment expecting to be called up. The streets of the city are about half a mile from the fort, and during the four or five following days troops of the rioters were to be seen, rushing from place to place plundering and burning. Day and night we manned the ramparts in the hot blasting sun, and day and night the guns and mortars belched forth, throwing shell and grapeshot, burning down houses, and scattering the demons wherever they were seen.

"We dared not leave the Fort, for who knows what the Sikhs would have done if it had been left empty? However, let us not breathe one word of suspicion against them, for they behaved splendidly, &c.

"The wicked 6th had marched out on the 7th, leaving two guns, and a Mussulman had set himself up in this city calling himself the agent of the King of Delhi, and calling on all natives, Hindoos, and true believers, to massacre all Europeans; and many poor fellows who had been in hiding fell into his hands and were murdered."

However painful it is to pursue this view of the horrors and atrocities of this mutiny at Allahabad, we must add to the above painful narrative an extract from the letter of the son of a clergyman to his father, dated "Chunar, June 6:"—

"And now I have a tale of fearful horrors to tell you of what happened at Allahabad. God grant it may be exaggerated; I fear it is too true. Let it stir up our English friends to send us with the utmost expedition the troops we so urgently require. On Saturday evening last, the 3d Oude Cavalry and 6th Native Infantry rose, and destroyed the bridge of boats, and murdered every European they could find. Out of seventeen officers at mess at 9.30, fourteen of them were butchered by 9.40, by the mutineers and mess-guard. And this is a regiment that volunteered to go against the Delhi rebels! Many of the poor residents had left the Fort, on account of the intense heat and the apparent security of everything. The mob and cut-throats rose with the soldiery. They burnt one whole family, from grandfather to grandchildren, alive! Others they killed by inches, cutting off the nose, then the ears, then fingers, then toes, &c. Children they killed, little innocent babes, before the mother's eyes, and then killed her!"

How fearful the exhibition, the confirmation, exhibited in the massacre and atrocities at Allahabad, at Cawnpore, and other places, of the representations of Holy Scriptures, that the heathen are "without natural affection," and the "dark places of the earth are filled with the habitations of cruelty." Of all cruelty to which man is impelled, none is greater than that which is called forth by *religious bigotry;* and to this we must trace what is occurring in India. The various reasons assigned for this fearful outbreak are for the most part mere pretexts. British dominion in India has proved the forerunner of civilisation, and most beneficent to the many millions thus placed under British sway. It is the success and wide-spreading influence of British Christianity shaking the superstitions of Hindooism and Mohammedanism—the diffusion of Christian knowledge by our schools for the instruction of the natives—the spread of railways, and other advances in civilisation,—these have excited in the minds of the Brahmins and Mohammedans the fear of the approaching downfall of their old superstitions and false religions, and of the final and near ascendancy of Christianity. Hence, though opposed to each other, Hindoos and Mohammedans combine together with maddened bigotry to uproot, to destroy, and to banish Christians and Christianity from India. A prophecy, long current among them, that British dominion in India was only to last for a hundred years, which period is now rapidly drawing to its close, may also have had its influence in hastening the calamities we now deplore. But however these events may for a time retard the progress of Christianity in our Eastern Empire, no one who believes the Word of God can doubt the ultimate triumphs of Christianity, and final downfall of all those systems of idolatry and superstition opposed to it. The present fearful events which are taking place in India, however painful and mysterious to us, we cannot doubt will be overruled by God to these grand ends. The ploughshare of war will break up and prepare the ground for the reception of the Word of eternal life, and thus will be hastened onward that glorious consummation for which every sincere Christian devoutly prays, when the Saviour of the world shall "receive the heathen for his inheritance, and the uttermost parts of the earth for his possession." How appropriate to the present times, and how consoling, is the prophetic language of Holy Scripture:—

"Why do the heathen rage, and the people imagine a vain thing? The kings of the earth set themselves, and the rulers take counsel together, against the Lord, and against his anointed, saying, Let us break their bands asunder, and cast away their cords from us. He that sitteth in the heavens shall laugh: the Lord shall have them in derision. Then shall He speak unto them in his wrath: and vex them in his sore displeasure. Yet have I set my king upon my holy hill of Zion. I will declare the decree:—the Lord hath said unto me,—Thou art my Son; this day have I begotten thee. Ask of me, and I shall give thee the heathen for thine inheritance, and the uttermost parts of the earth for thy possession. Thou shalt break them with a rod of iron; thou shalt dash them in pieces like a potter's vessel. *Be wise now therefore, O ye kings; be instructed, ye judges of the earth.*" (Psalm ii.)

CHAPTER III.

THE ESCAPE OF MARCUS CHEEK FROM THE MASSACRE—HIS SUFFERINGS—HIS HEROIC FAITH—HIS DEATH.

In the fearful outbreak and massacre of British officers and Europeans at Allahabad, what became of Marcus Cheek, our young Christian hero? Providentially on that night of horrors, when nine young ensigns were murdered by the treacherous Sepoys, whose dying shrieks were heard by the passers by, Marcus had left the mess-room at an early hour and retired to his own private lodgings. An overruling and merciful Providence thus rescued him from instant death, and preserved his life a few days longer, to fulfil his high commission of testifying his faith in his Saviour, and to strengthen others boldly to confess Christ in the face of cruel suffering and death. How the short interval was employed is known only to that God who seeth in secret. It was a time of seriousness, as danger was anticipated. It is no undue stretch of imagination to suppose that our young hero opened and read at that solemn evening hour that precious Bible his pious grandfather had given him before he quitted his English home, and that he prayed to the God of his fathers to prepare him for and protect him in anticipated trials and dangers. Soon the sound of sudden alarm, the rushing of multitudes, and the rattling noise of firing, roused him from reflection and rest. It is supposed that on leaving the house where he was, he was cut down by a Sepoy and left for dead. We must here give the few particulars which have been gathered in the words of his uncle, G. N. Cheek, Esq., communicated in a letter to his brother, the bereaved father:—

"*Bancoorah, June* 27, 1857.

"MY DEAREST OSWALD,—I have tried all in my power to get correct accounts regarding the death of your dear Marcus, and what I have obtained I have enclosed. You will see that after he was wounded he was left for days in the hands of the mutineers. Some accounts say that he must have had a little care taken of him, or he would not have lived so long; others say, the rascal of a landholder who had him neglected him, and the consequence was, when he was rescued and sent into the fort of Allahabad, he sank from exhaustion. Poor dear lad, he has been called early indeed to suffer. But it is a consolation to me (little though it may be to some), that he was not killed on the spot:—likely this short respite was given him to be more prepared to meet his God. Another comfort is, he had Christian burial: the others who were massacred were devoured by jackals and dogs; so in all your severe affliction your dear wife and self will have some little consolation. May He who can alone pour balm into your bleeding hearts abundantly bless and support you. The letters I enclose are all the information I can obtain to this date. I shall persevere and see if I can glean anything more, if so you shall have it.

"We have not come to a turn in our favour yet. Delhi is not taken. At Cawnpore and Lucknow we have great difficulty to hold our own, and shall not hold out long unless reinforcements reach these places. The deaths in Oude are fearful—not known yet in full. All India in a blaze! Prisoners let out of the gaols, and the treasuries robbed—more than a million and a-half of pounds sterling—besides stores taken by the rebels. We are in a fearful state; all the ladies from this have been sent into Calcutta—my dear wife gone too. Jane is coming down in the steamer to Calcutta. No civil station is safe. Here, at present, all is quiet, but in these days we may in an hour be attacked. I sleep with two revolvers loaded under my bed, and my gun loaded in my dressing-room. I hope my trust is in God, not in man; it is my duty to leave no stone unturned for defence, but results must be left to Him, who, though his providence may to us mortals be dark and mysterious, He does all things well: blessed be his holy name! My wife has suffered dreadfully on account of Marcus; she loved him and he loved her. I send a letter which came for him—it reached me after his death. I suspect it is from his dear mother. I have written to inquire about all the things Marcus had, and told them to sell nothing, but send all to me.

If I get anything I will send them to you, but I fear everything is gone."

Among the papers sent by the uncle is the following extract from "The Englishman," of Calcutta, June 24, 1857:—

"Cheek, a young ensign, who had been wounded when the rest of the officers of the 6th Regiment were shot down by the miscreants of that corps, came in to-day (to the Fort). He had been kept by a zemindar (a landholder), a known scoundrel, who starved him. Cheek is rapidly sinking, poor fellow, from exhaustion."

The uncle adds to this brief statement in his letter to the father:—

"Your noble boy was not only a soldier, but a Christian. The zemindar, into whose hands he had fallen, wanted the dear, dear departed lad to become a Mussulman, giving him the choice of doing so, *or death!* The noble lad replied, *'Anything but resign my faith and hope in my Redeemer!'* So, my brother, the noble boy died a martyr, and although his name may not be mentioned among those noted as martyrs, to all intents he was a blessed one. He, glorious boy, acknowledged Christ before Christ's enemies; and Marcus will be acknowledged by his Saviour in the realms of bliss; one, who though young, has fought the good fight and not denied the faith; to such a crown of glory is promised, and none of Christ's promises shall fail. I pray God, if in my grey hairs I am called on as he was, the Holy Spirit may be given me to act as he, dear lad, has done. I ask no more; then come life or death, it little matters. How much more impressive is the conduct of dear Marcus than ten thousand sermons. Let us, my brother, follow his example; let us be ready, as he evidently was, and then we shall meet him in glory!"

So far as can be gathered from the various accounts which have come to hand, our young hero, after he had been dreadfully wounded by a sabre cut on the night of the outbreak of the mutiny and massacre of the officers, was able to effect his escape and to hide himself, as the affecting notice of him in the "Times" states, in a ravine on the banks of the Ganges. "Here," as that notice says, "he found a stream, the waters of which sustained his life for four days and nights. Although desperately wounded, he contrived to raise himself into a tree during the night for protection from wild beasts. Poor boy! he had a high commission to fulfil, before death released him from his sufferings. On the fifth day he was discovered, and dragged by the brutal Sepoys before one of their leaders, to have the little life in him extinguished." (The leader before whom he was dragged appears to have been the Moulvie, the head of the insurgents.) "There," this account proceeds to state, "he found another prisoner, *a Christian Catechist*, whom the Sepoys were endeavouring to torment and terrify into a recantation. The firmness of the native was giving way, as he knelt amidst his persecutors, with no human sympathy to support him. The boy officer, after anxiously watching him for a short time, cried out, '*Oh, my friend, come what may, do not deny the Lord Jesus Christ!*'"

It was just at that critical moment the gallant Colonel Neile, with his heroic Madras Fusiliers, came to the deliverance of Allahabad and the beleaguered fort. The insurgents, with their leader, were put to flight, and the noble confessors at the Moulvie's head-quarters were mercifully delivered.

The following interesting letter communicated by the uncle will throw light on this statement and supply some very important, interesting particulars as to the sufferings, faith, and death of our young Christian martyr:—

"*Fort Allahabad, June* 19, 1857.

"MY DEAR MR. CHEEK,—I received this morning your letter of the 12th inst., and proceed to answer it as well as I can, and give you what particulars I have been able to obtain regarding poor Marcus Cheek's death. On the night of the 6th inst. he had left the mess-room before nine p.m. and gone to his own house, which was not far distant, and retired to rest. From that period till for four or six days afterwards nothing was heard regarding him, and it was supposed he had been killed amongst the many who fell victims to the treachery of the 6th Regiment. About the 12th we heard he was lying, badly wounded, at the Khowhs or Gardens, where the Moulvie, the head of the insurgents at Allahabad, had established himself. Holding the

Fort with so few men we could make no offensive movements, and could only hope that the poor survivors might yet remain alive when means were at our disposal to punish. On the 17th inst. the Moulvie fled in consequence of our small force moving out, and burning Durghabad and chasing the insurgents from Kydgunge, a portion of the native city; and in the same morning poor Cheek was brought into the Fort, having been sent from the gardens in a dooly to the American Mission-house, about a mile distant from the Fort, by some friendly people; from whence we brought him by sending some men of the Madras Fusiliers in a steamer up the Jumna river, the Mission-house being on its bank. Poor fellow, he was in a sad state, at times slightly sensible, and at times the reverse; but from what fell from his lips we believe that he was attacked in his own house, and in the attempt to escape was cut down at the door by a sabre cut across the brow or head, where he had a most severe wound. When he came among us he remembered nothing but the fact of some people having been kind to him and giving him water and melons; all else was confused. Evidently he had suffered much, and his body exhibited signs of great suffering in the marks of bruises and sores caused from exposure to the sun. He died the same evening, and was buried in the covered way of the Fort, near the river side, and at the salient angle of the Jumna battery. But if I am necessitated to be so open with you in detailing particulars of the manner of his death, I am happy, also, to be able to tell you of matters preceding which may comfort those to whom he was dear. A conductor of my establishment, a Mr. Coleman, and his wife, were seized by the insurgents and taken to the gardens, where they saw poor Cheek. Every effort was made by these rebels to induce them to abjure their faith and become Mohammedans, and threats were made, that, unless they did so, they must forfeit their lives. *Poor Cheek, in his almost last moments of sensibility, called Mrs. Coleman to his side, and bade her remember, and to do everything but that;—to be true to her faith and hope;* and after these few words of exhortation she and he were parted; and we know no more; but amidst the records of heaven these few words of his may have been written, and brought down a message of pardon and acceptance to the dying soldier.

. . . .

"W. C. Russell.

"P.S. I have just heard from another source that poor Cheek's last wish before he died, in a few moments of seeming consciousness, *was to write to his mother.*"

The following, from one of the American missionaries, of the name of Joseph Aben, addressed to Mrs. Cheek, will supply additional particulars:—

"*Allahabad, June* 23, 1857.

"My dear Mrs. Cheek,— Your kind letter of the 12th inst. has just reached me, the Benares *Dâk* having been closed up for several days. It is indeed pleasant to hear from friends once more. I have also just received a letter from my dear wife, giving me good accounts of her own and our dear boy's continued welfare. From the Cawnpore side we have had no dâk for about three weeks. You ask me about your dear nephew. On the night of the 6th instant, about nine o'clock, the 6th Regiment of Native Infantry broke out into mutiny, sounded an alarm, called the officers to the parade-ground, and then and there shot seven of their officers. Others were also wounded. Indeed, the number of Europeans and East Indians who were victims of the massacre amounts to about thirty. The incendiarism has been dreadful, far more destructive than at any other station; very few bungalows at our once large station have escaped. All our Mission property has been destroyed. I have lost all my private property, and a library which cost me about 10,000 rupees, but which no money can ever replace. I had a large collection of precious, old theological volumes, long since out of print, collected from various parts of Europe; also a large classical, and a German and an Oriental library of valuable books and manuscripts. The authorities would not allow me to take anything into the Fort, so I lost everything, except a few changes of clothes and a few volumes. We in the Fort heard the firing from cantonments shortly after nine o'clock at night, but for some time knew not the cause. Our chief apprehension had been regarding the arrival of mutineers from Benares, having heard that that station was in a blaze; but those mutineers never came. Our troubles came only from the loyal (!) 6th, who had offered their services to go and fight the rebels at Delhi, and who had at six o'clock in the evening of the 6th received the thanks of the Governor-General, at a special parade ordered for the purpose, and returned the same with three *hearty* cheers! Three hours afterwards they shot their officers! Of the seventeen who sat down to dinner at mess that evening, only three are known to survive, viz., Colonel Simpson, Captain Gordon, and Lieutenant Currie. Colonel Simpson's horse was riddled with bullets, but he managed to reach the Fort in safety. Lieut. Currie's horse was shot from under him, but he got another, and reached the Fort. Seven officers were shot on the parade ground, and their bodies were never recovered. Others were murdered elsewhere, and their bodies shared the same fate. Some of the bodies of the young ensigns were believed to be in the mess-house when that was burnt. A week ago to-day (Tuesday, 16th inst.) my mind was relieved by receiving a letter from our dear brother, *the Rev. Gopenauth Nundy*, regarding his safety. We had heard most distressing rumours about him. He said he was in the Mission school-house with *Ensign Cheek, and Conductor Coleman and his family.* On having escaped from the insurgents, *who had left the place that morning,* I went immediately to Mr. Court, the magistrate, who had just received a similar letter. I could not get writing materials, and, therefore, sent a verbal message that we would come immediately. We went up on a steamer, with a party of 100 Sikhs and 80 Fusiliers, and a 12-pounder, but met with no opposition. When we reached the place, they having misapprehended my message, had left. On returning to the Fort, I found Gopeenauth (Gopeenay) in my quarters. He and his wife and two children had been in the hands of the Mohammedans more than four days, and very badly treated. Immediately on our disaster here the Mohammedans set up a government of their own, which lasted nine days. They took the way of making converts which is peculiarly their own. Gopeenauth's feet were in the stocks four days and nights, and his wife was treated with great cruelty. On the night of the outbreak your nephew escaped to the Ganges, and was there found by the Mohammedans, and thence brought to their head-quarters. There Gopeenauth met with him, saw him wounded with sword-cuts, and showed him all the kindness in his power. The Mohammedans seeing this, separated them, and made Gopeenauth's feet fast in the stocks. Your nephew suffered greatly from thirst. Gopeenauth tried to get milk for him, but the Mohammedans prevented even this trifling kindness; nor would they allow him to give him a drink of water. Gopeenauth was enabled, by Divine grace, to witness a good confession. He publicly declared his faith before the scoffing Mohammedans; had worship with your nephew, and the other Christians who were with him, and showed that he was not ashamed of Jesus. He was frequently threatened with death by the Mohammedans, and told them he was not afraid! Your nephew said to him, '*Padre Sahib! hold on to your faith—don't give it up!*'

"On Tuesday, the 16th, after the party had reached the Fort, I was engaged in trying to make Gopeenauth and his family comfortable, and arranging for their immediate passage to Calcutta. While thus engaged I heard that young Cheek was very ill. Some one also said, that he had a relative living at *Bancoorah.* I instantly thought of you and Dr. Cheek, and without a moment's delay ran down to the hospital to see him. But it was too late; he was insensible, and died shortly afterwards. I never had the pleasure of his acquaintance, nor did I know, till too late to get a message from him, that he was related to you. After his recovery from the hand of the Mohammedan savages all was done for him that could be done; but his severe wounds, and exposure to the sun, and want of nourishment were too much for his physical frame. It will be a comfort to his friends to know that he received Christian burial from the Chaplain, the Rev. A. B. Spry, in the trenches of the Fort, on the morning of Wednesday, June 17th,—a blessing denied to many of his brother officers, whose bodies were never recovered after the massacre, and have probably been devoured by wild birds and beasts. These are mysterious dispensations of Divine Providence: but Jehovah reigns, and will doubtless bring good out of all this evil. *The movement appears to be a Mohammedan one; the cartridges are dexterously used as a handle for laying hold of the Hindoos.* "With best regards,

"Yours most sincerely,

"JOSEPH ABEN."

The remarks of the uncle, to whom these letters were addressed, in his letter to his brother in England, must not be withheld:—

"He (Marcus) is now clothed in white robes—the righteousness of his blessed Saviour—is crowned with the crown of glory. Happy Marcus! So soon taken from a world of sin and misery to a state of happiness in glory, and enjoying the presence of the Saviour, whom he boldly confessed before men. Do you not feel this, my brother and sister? Can you wish the beloved one back again? Does it not call for great thankfulness that he was permitted to show his faith in Jesus, while his comrades were killed on the instant? Think not of the sufferings the dear departed went through the few days he was in the rebels' hands; think of the manner in which he has glorified his God and Saviour, and of the happiness he is now enjoying, purchased through the blood of Christ, to whom be all the glory!"

A better idea will be formed of the amount of suffering endured by our young hero, of the strength of faith he displayed, and of the sustaining grace of God which supported him, from the following statement of the medical gentleman who attended him in his last hours. The letter is addressed to Dr. Cheek, of Benares :—

"*Allahabad, June* 30.

"MY DEAR CHEEK,—Your poor young cousin was brought into the fort in a very exhausted state between eleven and twelve o'clock on the 16th, and died a few minutes before four o'clock the same evening, and was buried in the fort. Brettingham and I saw him, and did all we could for him. *He had an incised wound over the right ear, through the scalp, an inch and a-half long; another in the left elbow, and left humerus fractured; his mind wandering; the skin was literally off his chest and thighs from exposure to the sun, &c., &c.*"

After the passing through the press of the former edition of this work, a letter was received by Mrs. Cheek (the mother), from the native teacher, *Goopenauth Nundy,* before mentioned, who is an ordained American missionary. This letter fully confirms the facts already related, and gives a fuller statement of the sufferings endured by our young Christian hero. The following extracts will be read with painful interest :—

"Next day, the 11th, your son was brought in as a prisoner about ten A.M.; he was led by two men holding his arm—not because he would run away, for he was too weak to do so, but to save him from falling down.

His wounds were many, but three were very severe: two in his head gaping about an inch, and one in his jaw-bone. They were all sword cuts. His only clothes which he had on him—a pair of trowsers and a flannel bannian—were, on account of the quantity of blood, as hard as a stone. He had no shoes or stockings; his uniform had been stripped off him. When he was brought into prison he was in a sinking state, and fell on the ground fainting. Finding poor Cheek in such a dreadful state of suffering, my heart yearned within me. I felt it my duty as a missionary, risking my life to assist the poor sufferer with any little thing in my poor. We had a little sutle and ghur, which I turned with a little water into a kind of gruel. Taking this, and drinking a full mud-pot of water, he felt greatly refreshed, and opened his eyes. I then went up to the Dareza (the jailor), and begged him hard to allow him a charpoy (a bedstead). The hard-hearted jailor condescended to grant my petition with the greatest reluctance; and though he gave a charpoy, it was a broken one,—their object was to see how much he could suffer. Ensign Cheek, finding me a fellow-prisoner, opened his heart at once to me, and told me the history of his sufferings. He took a most solemn promise from me, that if my life was spared—for he must have thought that he could not live—to write and acquaint you, and his aunt who was at Bancoorah, with the account of his sufferings and end."

The cruel jailor, seeing the kindness of the native

teacher to young Cheek, separated them, ordering the feet of the former to be fastened in the stocks. "To this," writes Goopenauth, "I made great resistance, and a body of rebels fell upon us with weapons, and forced my feet into the stocks, at the same time holding out the offer of release if I became a Mohammedan. They dragged my poor wife by her hair, which caused a severe wound in her forehead." It was at this moment and under these circumstances, as already related, our young Christian hero, in a short, emphatic sentence, exhorted the native teacher to hold fast his faith. "This small sentence," writes Goopenauth, "though it contains few words, was yet full of meaning. It was an expression of the speaker's heart, and of his love to our Saviour. I had no other opportunity of conversation with him on the subject of religion, but this free-will expression of these truly *strengthening* words—uttered, I may say, almost in the hour of death, makes me believe that he finished his course as a child of God. He is now enjoying eternal happiness in the mansions of glory.

"We were in the prison from Wednesday the 10th to Tuesday the 16th. All the time our sufferings were great indeed; for our food we received only a handful of parched grain in the midst of the day, and at night a single chopaty (a cake made of coarse flour, about 2 oz. in weight), which, I am sorry to say, your son was unable to eat, on account of the wound he had in his jaw-bone; the only thing he could swallow was a little milk, which was not given, though

I repeatedly begged, lying in the stocks. The Dareza was more cruel than his master, the Moulvie. Water was supplied only twice daily, and that sparingly. Poor Cheek, unable to eat the hard food, his only subsistence was water, which he was deprived of,—for hours and hours he used to cry for it.

"*Every few minutes a Mussulman used to come and threaten to cut off our noses and hands if we did not renounce our faith.*"

What, but strength from God, could have supported our young hero under such sufferings, during those four days and nights of solitary agony on the banks of the Ganges, and nerved him with such faith and endurance in the midst of scoffing and blood-thirsty Mohammedans, threatening him with death unless he denied his Saviour! We have in this evidence of God's faithfulness to his promise: "As thy day, thy strength shall be." He who calls his children to great trials and sufferings will impart special "grace to help in time of need." What striking proof have we of this in the case before us, and also in that of the martyrs. The weakness of youth and womanhood has waxed strong in the hour of trial, thus strengthened from on high. Weak humanity has never exhibited such super-human power, or appeared in more grandeur, than when thus called to the endurance of "cruel mockings," and cruel deaths for Christ. How many and how striking have been the instances of this during the late troubles and appalling atrocities!

The following extract from a letter of a dear friend, the wife of a Christian missionary, will supply proof of this:—

"*Bangalore, July* 20, 1857.

"MY BELOVED FANNY,—You will be anxious to have a line from us in these troublous times; and, just now, it is to us no small comfort that we have your sympathy and prayers. We cannot doubt that many a fervent supplication is ascending from our beloved country on our behalf, and for this sorely tried land; and may it not be in answer to these, coupled with those we have presented here, that hitherto we have been kept in safety?

"Since we last wrote, we have suffered the most painful alarm. Every day has brought tidings from the north of the most harrowing nature, either of fresh outbreaks, or of plots discovered, just in time to prevent their being executed; or of barbarities on the part of the mutineers only equalled by the atrocities of the North American Indians, or those fierce Fingoes in South Africa. We have been watching the increasing storm with the intensest anxiety,—and seeing it drawing nearer to us, until at last came this unwelcome truth, that it was around and among us. I cannot tell you the feelings with which we first realized this. Some of us felt that a natural death, or even being suddenly massacred, was a small thing compared to the indignities and lingering tortures which might await us. The great perfidy of the (native) troops, everywhere, made us feel safe at no moment. The Lord's people, at least many of them, drew together, and united in earnest prayer to Him who alone can protect and save us. We met, and still meet, in one of our school-rooms, at seven in the evening. The flushed cheeks and tears of the ladies, and the trembling voices of those (often officers) who lead our devotions, tell how deep is the general feeling. But these have already been seasons of much blessing. We have felt it good to unite in humbling ourselves before God, confessing our sins and the sins of our people, and have found our little strength renewed, and our hope and trust confirmed. We have been quite astonished to see how numerous were the portions of Divine truth just adapted to our peculiar position and circumstances. Some histories, which we before regarded as belonging to a past age, have contained such appropriate instruction and consolation that we have admired and blessed the wisdom that left them on record. One evening, dear Fanny, I shall long remember with thankfulness. In addition to alarming accounts in the papers, we had that day received letters from the different places, containing the most harrowing details. My dear husband and I felt extremely depressed; we felt that, before night was over, we and our beloved boy might be called to undergo similar treatment. We took the Bible, and read the Saviour's last instructions to his disciples in anticipation of the persecutions they would be called to endure; and as we lingered over and pondered his words of comfort, the Holy Spirit the Comforter came to us, removed the load that oppressed our hearts, and made us feel that we could accept anything with Christ and for Christ. May the love He has shown us in these times of trial bind our hearts more closely to Him!"

Such precious records of the faith and patience of many of our countrymen and countrywomen in India, shed a halo of heavenly glory over those trying scenes through which many of them have passed to that bright and better world, where they now experience "fulness of joy at God's right hand;" and "sorrow and sighing are for ever done away."

Such was the noble conduct of Marcus Cheek in the hour of trial and death. Who that contemplates this noble youth in the presence of cruel and scoffing Mohammedans, threatening him with torture and death unless he denied his Saviour, yet boldly confessing Him, and exhorting others to the same fidelity, can hesitate to enrol him in that "noble army of martyrs" who, "out of weakness were made strong, and waxed valiant in the fight" of faith? There is something touching in his last moments of consciousness, in the allusion of the dying youth to his *mother*. The last earthly desire which he expressed was to write to his *mother!* The love, the tenderness, the gratitude expressed in so touching a remembrance, breathes in it the spirit of Jesus, who in His last moments of unparalleled agony on the cross regarded his *mother* with affection, and cared for her comfort. To the sorrowing heart of the bereaved mother of our young martyr such a remembrance of her in such an hour may well prove a precious consolation in the season of her sorrow. Under whatever circumstances it may have been permitted to happen, "precious in the sight of the Lord is the death of his saints." It was the desire of an apostle "that Christ might be glorified in his body, whether by life or by death;" this privilege was granted to Marcus Cheek. A long life of distinguished piety and usefulness could not have glorified the Saviour more than our young Christian hero did by his stedfast, suffering, and triumphant faith in Christ, in suffering and dying hours. We must estimate life not by length of days, but by the fruits of faith, by which the Saviour is glorified. What though, as in the case of Marcus Cheek, the mortal remains of our beloved ones may slumber in distant lands, in unknown and unvisited graves, the Saviour watches over their sleeping dust; "they rest in their graves." Those graves contain precious "jewels," which Jesus purchased with His own blood. He will ransom them from the grave, and will claim and acknowledge them as his "*own*," in that day when He will "make up his jewels." The word of Christ abideth for ever: "Whosoever shall confess me before men, him will I confess also before my Father which is in heaven." (Matt. xi. 32.)

"His soul to Him who gave it rose,
God led it to his long repose,
Its glorious rest.
And though the Warrior's sun is set,
Its light shall linger round us yet,
Bright, radiant, blest."

Longfellow.

CHAPTER IV.

LETTERS OF SYMPATHY AND CONSOLATION TO THE PARENTS OF MARCUS CHEEK.*

SYMPATHY of man with man in joy and sorrow is one of those benevolent laws of human nature, implanted and provided by God for human happiness; for the increase of our mutual joys, and the mitigation of our mutual sorrows. How powerful and valuable is the manifestation of this sympathy at all times, but especially so in the hour of sorrow and bereavement! It is so universal, that we cannot behold sorrow in others without being in some measure touched with it ourselves. The tears of the bereaved parent appeal too strongly to the tenderness of our nature, and we can no more resist the contagion of grief, or be unmoved by the smile of rejoicing thankfulness, than the mirror refuse to give back the image placed before it, or the

* *The Author is bound to apologise to the sympathising friends whose letters are given in this chapter, for the liberty taken in publishing them, without previously asking their consent. His excuse must be the difficulty of obtaining the consent of so many parties, and his unwillingness to delay this publication a day longer than necessary.*

face of nature resist the glow of sunshine in the unclouded light of noon. The Christian religion, so wonderfully adapted to the wants of man's nature, as to assure us that He who made the one is the author of the other, supplies the most powerful motives to the exercise of this sympathy. It reveals to us the character of God, as "*the God of consolation.*" * "God that comforteth those that are cast down." † *He* hath given us in his holy Word, "many exceeding great and precious promises," all adapted to comfort us in the seasons of our sorrow. We have revealed to us a sympathizing Saviour, of whom we read that "He wept" at the grave of Lazarus, whom He loved; of whom the prophet declares, "He hath borne our griefs and carried our sorrows;" and who, though He hath passed into the heavens, and is far beyond the reach of sorrows, "can yet be *touched* with the feeling of our infirmities," because, when on earth, "He was in all points tempted and tried like as we are, yet without sin." ‡

"Touched with a sympathy within,
He knows our feeble frame;
He knows what sore temptations mean,
For He hath felt the same."

We have sympathizing friends, who "weep" with us when we weep, and "rejoice" with us when we rejoice. How grateful ought we to feel for this merciful provision made for our comfort—for that sympathy, which flowing through so many channels, cheers and sustains the mourner in times of sadness and affliction!

* Rom. xv. 5. † 2 Cor. vii. 6. ‡ Heb. iv. 15.

It has been the privilege of the bereaved parents of Marcus Cheek to experience this. The sufferings, faith, and death of their noble boy have awakened sympathy in thousands of Christian hearts, and called forth precious expressions of it in numerous letters to them, some of which the writer is privileged to transcribe. The following selection from the many before him, must suffice:—

LORD MARCUS HILL (TO THE FATHER).

"MY DEAR OSWALD,—I thank you much for the perusal of the several letters which I return. They are of no small interest to me in connexion with the early fate of my godson.

"What a melancholy gratification it is to know that he was so much appreciated.

"God give you all resignation and consolation!

"I am, very sincerely yours,

"*Aug.* 7." "A. MARCUS C. HILL.

THE EARL OF SHAFTESBURY.

"*Spa, Sept.* 14, 1857.

"SIR,—A letter from you to the Editor of the 'Times' reveals the name of that noble boy who died by the hands of assassins near Allahabad.

"I cannot repress the desire I feel to express my deepest sympathy with yourself, and my unbounded admiration of the heroism and conduct of your precious son.

"But we must do more than this;—we must (we, I mean every Englishman, nay, every true Christian)—we must give humble and hearty thanks to Almighty God, who raised up one of such tender years to bear such testimony, at such a time and in such circumstances. Surely, never were the words of the Liturgy more applicable: 'We also bless thy holy name for all thy servants departed this life in thy faith and fear; beseeching thee to give us grace so to follow their good examples, that with them we may be partakers of thy heavenly kingdom.'

"As a father, you must deeply feel the loss, for the flesh is strong; but as a Christian, you will rejoice to have been the father of such a child; and remember, too (we cannot see into futurity) that his end, had he lived longer, might not have been equal to his beginning. But now he is in everlasting security, beyond all the harm that might have reached him from the world, the flesh, and the devil.

"It is not given to many parents to produce such sons; and it is given to still fewer to have such complete and unmistakeable assurance that they are entered into their rest.

"You will excuse this intermeddling with your sorrows; but I have myself experienced something very similar; and I have the comfort of these considerations.

"I am, Sir, with much sympathy,

"Your faithful servant,

"SHAFTESBURY."

THE ARCHDEACON OF MEATH.

" *Archdeaconry, Kells, Ireland,*
Sept. 13, 1857.

"DEAR SIR,—Your loss is one that must engage the sympathy of thousands whom you can never know. Will you permit a stranger to express it?

"When the great and good Duke of Ormond heard of the death of his brave son, fighting against an enemy as barbarous as Sepoys, he exclaimed, 'I would not exchange my dead son for any living son in Christendom.'

"Where could this apply so well as to one who has early won his heavenly crown, with a spirit so unsubdued by suffering, so faithful unto death?

"But the expression needs some change for him. He is not dead, but liveth unto God.

"I thank God that his words have been preserved, to be an example to many, and I trust a comfort to yourself.

"I remain, with sincerest sympathy,
"Your faithful servant,

"EDWD. A. STOPFORD,
"Archdeacon of Meath."

THE HON. AND REV. BAPTIST W. NOEL, M.A.,

ON THE DEATH OF ENSIGN CHEEK, AND FIVE OTHER YOUNG ENSIGNS, MURDERED AT ALLAHABAD (AGED SEVENTEEN).

"Treason in Delhi's walls had risen;
Bengal's battalions rose;
And every fort became a prison
Begirt with Sepoy foes.

"Throughout the lines of Allahabad
Fanatic fury grew;
And mutineers, with hatred mad,
Their own commanders slew.

"One only from the gory heap
Crept out to die alone;
He did not wail, nor groan, nor weep,
But said, 'Thy will be done!'

"Within the covert of a wood,
Close by a streamlet's play,
Wounded and destitute of food,
Four days the soldier lay.

"And now they find him 'midst the trees—
Not friends who bring relief—
But Sepoys, who with fury seize
And drag him to their chief.

"One brandishes a bloody knife;
All hate to Christians bear;
Fresh stabs will take his ebbing life—
New curses wound his ear.

"But who is he that elder man,
Bound, beaten, fearing worse,
On whom each fierce Mahommedan
Is pouring out his curse?

"Why are those guards around him set?
Those cords upon his wrist?
He *was* the slave of Mahomet,
And *now* he preaches Christ.

"'Repent!' exclaimed the Sepoy crew,
'Or Allah's vengeance taste!'
'Repent!' exclaimed their Captain too,
'Or this day is thy last!

"'Seek then the prophet's aid by prayer,
Abjure the Christian lie;
Or by his sacred name I swear,
Apostate, thou shalt die!'

"The drops are standing on his brow,
His quivering lips are pale;
Who will sustain his weakness now,
For hope and courage fail?

"Then spake the wounded boy, while faith
Lighted his languid eye:
'O Brother! ne'er from dread of death
Thy Saviour's name deny!'

"Trembling no more, no more afraid,
The prisoner hears them crave;
Those words, that dying look, have made
His faltering spirit brave.

"'Hark! hark! it is the tramp of men;
The Fusiliers are here!'
And, rushing headlong down the den,
The Sepoys disappear.

"The Teacher clasped his hands with joy,—
'We are saved!—Our foes are fled!'
And then he turned to bless the boy,—
The heroic boy was dead!

"They bore his placid corpse away,
And dug a quiet grave
Far from his childhood's home, which lay
Across the Western wave.

"But ye who love him still shall greet
Your loved one once again;
For all who trust in Jesus meet
Beyond the reach of pain!"

B. W. N.

THE REV. DR. WILLIAMSON.

"*Pershore Vicarage, Sept.* 26, 1857.

"DEAR SIR,—I hope you will not think that I intrude too soon, stranger as I am, upon your domestic sorrow, if I send you a few words expressive of my deep sympathy with you in the loss of your son in India.

"I do not know when I have read so touching a story, as given in the newspapers, as his, poor boy! And that noble confession of faith with which he closed his life, when he encouraged his fellow-sufferer to stand firm, and not to deny his Lord—as one cannot read without tears. Surely, if the recollection of his heroism and truth can soften the grief which his loss must cause you, you have that consolation abundantly granted you, by his and your common Saviour.

"I am, dear Sir, with much respect,

"Yours faithfully,

"R. WILLIAMSON."

FROM A LADY.

"SIR,—I trust you will excuse a stranger for intruding upon you in your time of poignant sorrow, by writing a few lines of sincere and heartfelt sympathy. No one in our domestic circle could read the touching details of your noble son's steadfast faith and manly fortitude, amid his solitary and acute sufferings at Allahabad, without shedding tears. We wept when we thought of the lonely, mourning hearts of his parents, bereaved of such a son, so worthy of being the object of the warmest parental affection; and even then, there were mingled tears of holy joy with those of sorrow, as we thought on the bright transition to his pure emancipated spirit, as it winged its flight from the dreary scenes of rapine and bloodshed, to the sheltering arms of that compassionate and sympathizing Saviour, to whom he had been firmly "faithful unto death." The crown of life now gleams on his purified brow; he has 'washed his robes, and made them white in the precious blood of the Lamb.' In the lonely ravine, where his last suffering days were past, I believe many thoughts of his far distant home would come over his weary spirit, and perhaps the blessed memory of instruction received *there* in happier days might contribute, under God's blessing, to the completion of the work of sanctification within him and to his final ripening for glory. The last efforts of his expiring nature were given in his Redeemer's cause! Oh, Sir!

what comfort to you in thinking of this fact. Among all the incidents which I have read from India not one has touched my heart with the same interest as that of your dear son. Do excuse my boldness in writing. I have five sons; one dear daughter is, I believe, in the same bright land with your precious departed one; therefore my heart would mingle its sympathy in your grief. My husband begs also to join me in this, and commending you to Jesus' care and love,

"I remain, faithfully yours,

"ELIZA BANKS THOMSON."

AN INCIDENT IN THE WAR.

(*From the "Essex Herald."*)

OH earth, earth, earth! thy loud deep cry,
Full of intensest agony,
Comes mourning o'er the surging wave,
With shrieks for succour from the brave;
Thy sunlit morn, thy midnight air,
Echo the fever of despair;
Thy social fabric rent and riven,
Breathes its sad prayer for help from heaven.
Resting upon yon Christian's doom,
One brightening ray pervades the gloom;
It permeates his earthly night,
With beams of everlasting light.
Weary, exhausted, faint, and worn,
In frantic demons' battle storm;
He sees a little streamlet play
With the frail insect of a day,—
And slowly drags his sinking frame

To the cool current of the plain;
Where, sinking on the blood-stained sod,
He bathes his lips and seeks his God.
  Night closes round, too well he knows
Darkness releases other foes—
Foes framed by nature to be wild;
The forest and the jungle child.
He finds a shelter in a tree,
And from their hungry jaws is free;
But man, far fiercer than the beast,
Seeks in his Christian blood a feast,
And gloats with fiendish joy his eyes
Upon the hapless youth his prize;—
His weakened limbs, resistless now,
Before his heathen conqueror bow;
In very helplessness he yields,
Nor dares to show the scorn he feels,
But what to him the road he treads,
While God his soul with manna feeds?
His earthly home, his youthful life,
Must pay the penalty of strife;
Death's shadow, like a veil of love,
Gently descending from above,
Is hovering near to strike a blow,
To free him from his tyrant foe.
Yet stay, poor youth, one trial more
Awaits thee, ere thy mission's o'er;
Thou hast an aged Christian friend,
On whose pale, quivering lips suspend
The name of his new worshipped Lord,
The hatred of the Hindoo horde;
By cruel tortures he must die,
Or Jesus' blessed name deny.
  Oh, in this struggling conflict, Lord,
Do Thou thy strength and grace afford;
Give vigour to that feeble youth,
That he may plead the cause of truth.

He gently whispers in his ear,
"Behold by faith a Saviour near."
He pleads that Saviour's suffering name,
And bids the aged man proclaim
To heathens, that "He dies to live
In bliss which Christ alone can give."
He needs no more; that living faith
Invests him with a hope in death;
Then turns to bless the Christian boy
Who fills his dying ears with joy;
But he is not; the spirit band
Had borne him to a happier land;
And through that night the old man's dream
Was full of Jesus' precious theme,—
"Whoso on earth confesses me
Will I confess eternally."

ALPHA.

FROM A LADY.

"HONOURED SIR,—I must honour the parent of the young hero, saint, and martyr of Allahabad, in proportion to the reverence I feel for his son, in common with *all* who have or shall read the details of his *most glorious* and *triumphant death,* supported and supporting another with his latest breath, by his most holy faith, amidst sufferings and terrors at which the stoutest hearts might quail. Yours is indeed a rich consolation; your soldier of Christ promoted to 'the holy army of martyrs,' whom we reverently remember in our Church prayers! May we all be given grace to follow their good examples!

"But I must, as a perfect stranger, apologize for

the liberty I have taken in addressing you. *A very dear godson of mine was a fellow-voyager with your precious son, reached that ill-fated station one day before him, and would, on this day, have completed his eighteenth year. He fell on that sad 6th of June, but how, or when, we cannot learn,* and the accounts of that dreadful night given in the papers are so vague and various, that his poor parents and friends are constantly torn by the conflicting accounts given, without knowing which to believe. His name was Thomas Lane Bayliff; and if in any letters you may have, his *untimely* and *much lamented* death is mentioned, you would confer a great favour on the writer and his sorrowing and bereaved family, by letting me know any particulars of his melancholy fate which may have reached you. He, too, was a jewel; but few find grace *early* or *late* to *shine with lustre* such as your dear lost son's. May the God of consolation support you under your bereavement!

"I have the honour to be, yours, &c.,

"E. B. LANZEEN."

FROM A LADY.

"DEAR SIR,—Will you accept this poor expression of a stranger's sympathy with your sorrow and your consolation?—

"THE LAST BREATH.

"Dark faces thronged around them,
Beneath an Eastern sky;
Two helpless captives hunted forth
To suffer and to die.

"Dark faces swarmed around them,
Raging with hate and scorn;
They stood amid a host of foes,
Weak, wasted, and forlorn.

"The one, an English stripling,—
What thoughts are with him there?
His father's blessing on his head—
His mother's parting prayer.

"So late, their tears and kisses
Seem warm upon his brow!
Their voices murm'ring in his ear—
Oh! could they see him now!

"And one, a swarthy native
Who, in some hour of need,
Had learned to serve a holier God,
And teach a purer creed.

"Well might his spirit falter,
Well might his heart be wrung;
The taunts and curses heaped on him
Were in his native tongue.

"The memories of his childhood,
The friendships of his youth—
Life, home, and freedom proffered still,
Would he but spurn the truth.

"What marvel if that moment
A wavering thought might crave—
An aching doubt, Is mine a God
Who will not smite or save?

"But clear above the tumult
Arose a warning word
In English accents,—'Oh, my friend,
Deny not Christ the Lord!'

"And, strengthened for endurance,
He gazes on the foe—
Yet, hark! what mean those rushing sounds?
Well do the traitors know!

"Nearer the tramp of horsemen!
Nearer that ringing shout!
And wild, wild yells of baffled rage,—
They flee in headlong rout.

"The rescued native utters
A cry of thanks and joy;
But mute and lifeless at their feet
Lies the brave English boy!

"Sees not the friendly faces,
Hears not the victor's cheer;
But who may tell what sights or sounds
Woke on his eye and ear?

"The faithful, the true-hearted—
Far shall his tale be heard;
His spirit had departed,
E'en with the warning word."

FROM A LADY.

"*9th September*, 1857.

"MY DEAR SIR,—As human sympathy seems the best consolation in sorrow, next to the comfort which we know will be bestowed by a gracious God upon those whom He has permitted to suffer affliction for some hidden good to those who trust in Him, I cannot forbear telling you that I know a wide circle wherein your noble son has been distinguished above all the sufferers in this dreadful time of crime and sorrow.

"We think the faith which shone so brightly in your son's fearful trial must have been learnt at the home he had so recently left.

"The faith which supported the son will, I trust, enable the father to seek and obtain comfort from whence only it can be obtained.

"Sincerely wishing that your eldest son may return in safety,

I remain,

"THE MOTHER OF AN OFFICER NOW BEFORE DELHI."

FROM A LADY.

"*Richmond-hill, Surrey.*

"SIR,—I have sent you by this day's post a little book, entitled 'Gone Home to be with Jesus.' It is out of print, so you must excuse its being dirty. It may interest you to hear that an excellent discourse was preached on the account given of your son (I was told) at Marylebone Church, on Sunday last. The little book is on the death of a child, but will, I trust, comfort you. What are all the sufferings of the body—the shell—compared to the triumphs of the emancipated spirit? My own heart is mourning the loss of a darling child, so I can feel for you under your acuter affliction. But how glorious was your noble boy's death after all!—glorious in the sight of angels and the Great Redeemer, whose faith he confessed, and who will not deny him when He comes again in the clouds of heaven attended by all his saints.

"Yours sympathizingly,
"JULIA A. BARRETT."

BY THE SAME.

"LINES ON THE NOBLE YOUNG OFFICER AT ALLAHABAD.

"Those were well-spoken words, young Ensign brave—
'Deny not' Him who died thy soul to save!
'Deny not' Him who suffered pangs untold!
Oh! '*Come what may,*' the faith of Christ uphold!
Thy mission was fulfilled, thy Lord was nigh;
Angels rejoiced, and wafted thee on high!
For ever free from all thy foes and fears,
Jesus will thee confess 'when He appears!'

"J. A. B."

FROM A LADY.

"SIR,—Your great grief is borne upon thousands of hearts in this country; but condolence for your natural distress must mingle with high congratulations in being the father of a Christian hero, who, having proved himself 'a child of God' upon earth, is now (we may not doubt it) an 'inheritor of the kingdom of heaven.'

"I venture to beg your acceptance of two copies of the accompanying stanzas, to the memory of your son.

"I remain, Sir, with much sympathy, &c.,

"RACHEL ELIZ. CRESSWELL.

"*Bank House, King's Lynn,*
Sept. 10, 1857.

"THE YOUTHFUL MARTYR.

"Four weary nights and days,
In danger and distress,
By the river brink he laid,
In utter helplessness.

"He hears the wild beasts' howl,
And the jackal prowling nigh;
But 't is music to the sound
Of the Sepoys' cry.

"The boy was scarce sixteen
When he left his parents' side
For India, with her storied pomp,
And her military pride.

"A few short, busy months!
Bleeding and wounded, he,
By the mutineers in Allhabad
Unseen, in misery,

"Crawls from the crimson field,
Drinks of the running stream,
Then sinks exhausted, slumbers,
And dreams—'t is all a dream!

"He has nobly done his work,
Nor grudged his young life-blood;
For the mother and the children
To the death he stood.

"Now life is ebbing fast;
But he deems the hour blest,
When, on his Saviour's bosom,
He shall sink to rest.

"Not yet, not yet, young hero!
Though thy work be well nigh done,
There is a nobler deed before thee,
Ere the victory be won!

"The fiendish traitors find him,
They drag him to their lair—
A man in tortured agony
Is writhing there.

"It is a Christian convert,
Not daring to deny
The Lord of life and glory,
And yet afraid to die.

"With promises of freedom, life,
They ply their victim still;
But death, in every hideous shape,
If he refuse their will.

"Oh! 'twas a fearful moment!
A soul endangered then—
The immortal for the mortal
Perilled from fear of men.

"There is a hush, a stillness;
For a voice, soft, calm, and clear,
Issues from lips so deadly white—
The murderers pause to hear:

"'Oh! whatsoe'er you suffer—
Oh! whatsoe'er you do,
Deny not Christ the Saviour,
The Lord who died for you!

"'T is past! the sound has died away,
Drown'd in the war cry loud
Of British warriors, bursting
Upon the murd'rous crowd.

"The rescued convert turns to bless,
And for the boy to pray;—
He needs it not! the victory's won—
The spirit has passed away!

"R. E. C."

THE REV. M. M. HUMBLE.

"*Sutton Rectory, Chesterfield,*
Sept. 11, 1857.

"SIR,— * * * *
* * * * *

"I feel impelled to express to you, in however feeble a way, my intense admiration of your child's Christian courage and example, and, at the same time, my real sympathy with you as a sorrowing parent. And yet, let me say, Why sorrow in the way and to the extent named in your letter? Will not your noble son be numbered with the glorious army of *martyrs?* And what an honour is *that* to *him,* the coming *crown* making even more bright and blessed the rest and light of paradise,—and to you, the instrumental author of his existence! Had he been spared to you on earth, could any worldly honour—any princely preferment—any, the highest, place in the kingdoms of this world, have given him such a position as he now holds in the

'Peerage' Book of the King of kings? Though 'sorrowing,' yet surely you can and will 'rejoice.' I only know that I have read of your son's confession unto death as though I were carried back to the apostolic age; and, whilst I sympathize with your sorrow as a parent, I rejoice and am thankful that out of the evil and misery of this cruel Indian rebellion the Great Head of the Church has brought to light *such* a *witness* (the literal meaning of the word martyr) to His truth and the power of His grace,—and that at a time when faith so much fails, and love is growing cold."

TO THE MOTHER.

"'SORROW NOT AS THOSE THAT HAVE NO HOPE.'

" 'T was not a cruel hand that tore
  Thy blossom from the bough,
And traced another line of woe,
  Bereaved one, on thy brow.

"The sever'd cord will be reknit,
  That wrung thy heart's deep core,
Where shears of death can enter not,
  And life is evermore.

"There was a scar upon his brow,
  The farewell mark of death;
It changed into a martyr's crown,
  A holy victor's wreath.

"Thou scarce hadst deem'd the grain was ripe
  To harvest it so soon;
Thou scarce hadst deem'd the morning full,
  When, lo! the light of noon.

"Scarce was the earth-light kindled, when
Its flame was fast a-gone;
But death could not extinguish it;
For, lo! a star it shone.

"Thou would'st not have him fading here
'Mid earth's cold winds and showers,
Rather than blooming even now
'Mid Heaven's gathered flowers.

"Then deem not thou as sad the life
That had so short an even:
Think of his martyr glories now—
A chosen one of heaven.

"Think of thy hero, not thy boy—
Thine angel, not thy son;
And let thy worn heart yearn to know
The heaven he hath won.

"And yet we cannot still the sigh,
Forbid the dropping tear—
He was too bound to us, too close,
Too well-belov'd, too dear.

"Oh! may the God that claimed His own
Be near thee in thy sorrow!
Life is but short—thy martyr'd son
Shall greet thee on the morrow.

"LIZZIE FOSTER."

"*Evesham.*"

FROM A LADY.

"*Westow Hall, York, Sept.* 16.

"SIR,—I hope that even a stranger may venture to

offer to you some expression of the deep sympathy with which she—in common, doubtless, with thousands—has read that most touching account of the manner in which it has pleased God that you should be deprived of a most noble son. Deep, indeed, must be the anguish of his parents and friends; and yet surely, dear Sir, you have the highest consolation in your intensity of grief. Is it not blessed indeed to think that you had been enabled *so* to bring up your child as he must have been brought up, and to think that at an age so early he should have been permitted to win the martyr's glorious crown?

"A few days ago, I met with a passage relating to the unspeakable horrors of this Indian war, which I thought so beautiful and so consoling that I copied it, and now I will venture to send it to you. I should be indeed thankful if it should bring you any thought of comfort:—

"'One thought, and one alone, can give any support to the mind when these agonizing scenes are forced upon it. There was One Spectator, whose thoughts are not as our thoughts, and in whose eyes every pang, every indignity, borne in submission to His will, was no stain or pollution, but a fresh claim to glory. And among the sufferers there may have been those who were supported by something above ordinary Christian patience, by the knowledge that as by their labours in his service they had not feared to risk the most fiery persecution, as in his service they did not refuse to suffer it,—so He was admitting them through this gate of brief but terrible anguish, to a place in that glorious rest under the altar reserved for those "which were slain for the Word of God and the testimony which they held," to cry out till their number is accomplished, "How long, O Lord!"'

"Many, many are the daily prayers offered for the *mourners*, among whom you are now included; and little children join in these prayers. I have just now been hearing a dear boy, *Arthur*, and his little sister, repeat their prayers, and one prayer is for our countrymen in India, adding the words, 'Comfort all their friends, and bring all at length to heaven!'

"May our most loving Lord, who 'healeth the broken in heart and giveth medicine to heal their sickness,' heal and comfort you and yours, and give you at length a blessed meeting with the beloved one whom you have *not* lost!

"Allow me to remain, dear Sir,

"Yours in true sympathy,

"SARAH DONKIN."

LINES TO THE MEMORY OF THE LATE ENSIGN CHEEK.

"'How is he numbered among the children of God, and his lot among the Saints.'—*First Evening Lesson for All Saints' Day*.

"Basking in the light of summer,
England saw the red bolt fall,
And the plenteous joys of harvest
Quench'd by tidings from Bengal.

"Then too came the mournful story
Of a youthful hero's death,
With his holy breast-plate round him,
Couch'd upon the shield of faith.

"Thinking of his pleasant childhood,
And his parents' sadden'd years,
We a little while kept silence,
For we could not speak for tears;

"And we said, such grief is sacred,
Let no careless foot intrude
On the holy ground of sorrow,
Till its anguish be subdued.

"When the months have faded slowly
We will give a song for him,
With the music of our dirges
Blending rapture's loftiest hymn,—

"Turning with a deep thanksgiving
From his grave beneath the sod,
To the happy saints that slumber
'In the faith and fear of God.'

"Only such high song of triumph
Should be poured above the dead
As exulting angels chanted
When the early martyrs bled; '

"When, like parting sunlight, falling
Swiftly on the dying year,
Comes that day of pure rejoicing
Many a striving heart to cheer.

"We departed saints remember,
'Meekly kneeling on our knees.'
Oh, thou young and brave confessor,
Come and take thy place with these!

"With immortal hope to cheer thee,
  Strong the waves of death to stem,
Thou wert tempted, slain, tormented—
  Come and share the crown with them.

"Witnessing a good confession,
  With a courage high and calm,
Comforting a wavering brother,
  Thine shall be the victor's palm.

"Rest—thy burning thirst is over,
  All thine agony and pain;
Thou hast quaffed the living water,
  And shalt never thirst again.

"D. S. W.

CHAPTER V.

CONCLUDING REMARKS.

The preceding memorials of the early life, sufferings, faith, and death of Marcus Cheek, suggest some important remarks, which will form a suitable conclusion to this work.

We see *the importance of having the mind well instructed and established, in early life, in the principles of the religion of Christ.* The season of childhood and youth is the best time for sowing the seed of religious instruction. The mind is then most tender, more susceptible of religious impression, and more free from those evil principles by which advancing youth is sure to be assailed; and thus, with the blessing of God, becomes fortified and strengthened against temptations. To withhold religious training from the child, is to launch inexperienced youth on a treacherous ocean, without rudder or compass, the sport of every wind that blows, to be driven on the rocks or engulphed in the deep. Religious principles implanted in childhood are the *seeds* of future excellence and usefulness. They may be long buried, and may be thought to be lost; but though in some cases it may be so, yet we know that, unless the seed be sown at the proper season, there can be no harvest. Though, for a time, the field may give no promise of fruitfulness, it is a ground of hope that the seed *has* been sown—that the seed *is* there. It is a further ground of hope that the Divine promise assures us of the blessing: "In due time ye shall reap if ye faint not." The time will arrive in which it will be manifest that religious principles, early imparted, have been the seeds of those excellencies which are developed in after years,—that thus the mind has been trained and moulded for new and untried circumstances, and strengthened to resist temptation, to endure affliction, to bless others, and to glorify God. Let parents and guardians of our youth, by assiduous religious teaching, and with earnest prayer, thus implant religious principles, and right practice and religious fruitfulness will be the result. If they neglect this, and yet expect that our youths will be virtuous and holy, they are guilty of the folly of those who expect to reap the harvest, but have neglected to sow the seed. What pleasing proof of this have we in the case of *Marcus Cheek.* His voluntary dedication of himself to God in *Confirmation* at Brussels, his own desire to renew that dedication at the Lord's Table, on the first opportunity that offered on his return to England, are proofs of this. The religious principles implanted in childhood, developed their vitality and efficacy in India, sustaining him in the time of suffering, and nerving him with Christian courage, rather to die for Christ than to deny Him.

Oh, that like *Marcus Cheek,* every young reader of this work were persuaded, and enabled by Divine grace, to give up the heart early to God, and to walk in his ways. Such know not the future circumstances of their coming days,—what temptations, what trials, what dangers, are before them. The only sure way to happiness, to safety, and comfort, under trouble,—to courage and support in the face of peril and death, is, in sincerity and prayer, early to give up the heart to God and his service.

We have in the narrative of *Marcus Cheek* an instructive instance of *the value and power of living faith in God, to sustain under suffering and give courage in death.* Where we see the *fruits* of faith, we cannot doubt its reality and vitality. It is one principle end and use of biography, especially of religious biography, to show us how men of like passions with ourselves have acted in difficult circumstances, and to develop the principles by which they were influenced and sustained. There are some situations and circumstances in life in which some deem it next to impossible to maintain real dignity and consistency; but holy Scriptures, which are adapted for all conditions of life, and furnish rules and examples for conduct under all difficulties, record how Joseph and Daniel served God and benefitted their fellow-creatures when captives to heathen masters. The unlooked-for calamities which have overwhelmed our countrymen in India may have been in many cases rendered yet more dreadful by the idea of the difficulty of retaining true dignity and honour in such circumstances; and brave men and high-minded women, fearing shame more than death, may be almost tempted to despair and desperation rather than fall under the power of their enemies. Such despair and desperation are both alike equally forbidden by the lessons and examples of holy Scripture. Living faith in God is the best and only sure preservative in these temptations and dangers. The concluding verses of that history of the power of faith recorded in Heb. xi. 32—40 show us what *great* things faith can *do* and *suffer*. The case of Daniel and his young companions in Babylon seems recorded on purpose to meet such cases as are now occurring in India, and such as that in which Marcus Cheek was placed. Daniel and his companions resisted the temptations from the royal table: thus commencing their brilliant course with that *self-denial* which was the foundation of future greatness, by perseverance in the strictest temperance, and maintaining the habit of prayer even when it exposed them to danger and death. May we not remark the pleasing indication of this in the fact of Marcus Cheek's early retirement from the mess-room, on the fatal night, to his own house, most likely for meditation and prayer? We mark in Daniel and his companions, when tempted and threatened to deny God by an act of idolatry, how living faith in God sustained and triumphed! When threatened with a fearful death unless they bowed down to worship the idol, what fidelity to God, what true heroism, is shown in their firm reply:—"If it be so, our God whom we serve is able to deliver us from the burning fiery furnace, and He will deliver us out of thine hand, O King. But if not, be it known unto thee, O King, that we will not serve thy gods, nor worship the golden image which thou hast set up!"* Here is the power and triumph of living faith in God. Such was the faith of *Marcus Cheek*, when threatened with death unless he denied his Saviour: "*Anything but give up my faith in my Redeemer!*" was his noble reply, and such was the faith to which he exhorted and encouraged others. Noble boy! thy example speaks to a thousand hearts the power of faith to impart true courage and triumph in hours of suffering and death! May the youths of your loved native land learn from thy example the necessity and value of living faith in God, to protect them in the hour of temptation, to deliver them in peril; and then, whatever may befall the fleshly tabernacle, their spirits will be happy and safe; for "the souls of the righteous are in the hand of the Lord, and there shall no torment touch them." Such a faith, founded in assured belief of the Divine promises, and a realizing sense of the Divine presence, takes firm hold of the strength of the Almighty, and gives unearthly support and triumph in danger, suffering, and death.

We learn also from the case of Marcus Cheek *the duty and honour of boldly confessing Christ before men.* The case of Daniel and his companions, before referred to, is one among many instances to show that such courage and heroic faith, contrary to the ideas of some

* Daniel iii. 17, 18.

timid and unfaithful professors, is crowned with respect and even temporal advancement; for we read, "Then the King *promoted* Shadrach, Meshach, and Abed-nego, in the province of Babylon!"* Nothing is lost, even in a temporal point of view, by fidelity to God and his service. But we must take higher ground. Such the promise of the Saviour sets before us:—"Whosoever, therefore, shall confess me before men, him will I confess also before my Father (and before the angels of God) which is in heaven."† The connexion in which this promise is found clearly points to similar circumstances as those in which Marcus Cheek confessed and honoured the Saviour. "Fear not them which kill the body, but are not able to kill the soul: but rather fear Him which is able to destroy both body and soul in hell; whosoever shall confess me before men, him will I confess also before my Father which is in heaven." How glorious the promise! When our young hero sunk in weakness into the arms of death, the Saviour, whom he boldly confessed, received his emancipated spirit and confessed him before his Father. And when the Saviour shall come again "in glorious majesty" to raise his sleeping saints He will confess before an assembled universe Marcus Cheek as one of that "noble army of martyrs," who thus honoured him "before men." Marcus has received from his Saviour the martyr's crown: for He hath said,—"Be thou faithful unto death, and I will give thee the crown of life!" But how fearful the alternative:—"Whosoever

* Dan. iii. 30. † Matt. x. 32; Luke xii. 8.

shall deny me before men, him will I also deny before my Father which is in heaven!"

The present fearful state of India and its future prospects cannot, in conclusion, properly pass unnoticed. British dominion there has now existed for nearly 100 years. Though its beginning was small, its increase and extension by conquest and cession is extraordinary. That so mighty an empire, with a population of little short of *two hundred millions* of Hindoos and Mohammedans, should have been brought under British sway, is in itself indicative of some great design of Providence to be accomplished by this country for the welfare of India. This design will not be overlooked or mistaken by a Christian people. It was not that Britain might be enriched by the treasures of the East; but that India might receive from her what is far more necessary and valuable, "the unsearchable riches" of the knowledge of a Saviour; not that Britain might be aggrandised by an Empire, on which it is vauntingly said, "the sun never sets," but that India might be added to the kingdom of our Lord Jesus Christ. It is for this high and holy object British dominion has been established in India; our tenure of India depends upon our fulfilment of this high trust and destiny. It is by Evangelizing India we can only hope to civilize her. Our duty as a Christian nation and Church to attempt this is not doubtful or optional, but clear and imperative. The Saviour's command, that his Gospel shall be preached in "all nations," and compassion for the souls of the millions held under cruel and debasing superstitions, demand this of Christian Britain. Alas! how little has been done by us to fulfil this great duty of christianizing India. The *aggregate* of *all* Christian efforts and success is thus summarily stated:—

"Missionaries have been established in more than 300 stations throughout India: mission-schools have amounted to the number of 2,015. There have been nearly 80,000 children in these schools. Missionaries have itinerated in all directions, singly and in company, with native Christians, and nearly 80,000 Christian converts have been made in Southern India."

But great as this effort and success may appear, and full of promise as it is for the future, it is mostly the result of the Divine blessing on the *voluntary* efforts of the Christian Church. *The Government,* whether at home or abroad, has made no decided effort *as a Government* for the religious instruction and conversion of the millions of its heathen subjects in India. It has established the Eastern Episcopacy, and provided chaplains for the English residents, its military and civil officers; but as a professedly *Christian* nation and Government no provision has been made for the conversion of the heathen. On the subject, the remarks of the Bishop of Durham, in a speech delivered lately at Durham, will find an echo in thousands of hearts. The Bishop expressed regret "to be obliged to say that he thought England, in all her dealings with her empire in India, had not been true to the Christian principles and faith she professed. He did feel they had been over-indulgent in dealing with the hideous superstitions which pervaded that land. They had given, *as a Government*, their full confidence and support to the idolatrous religions of the country, while, as a Government, they had given no encouragement to the propagation of the Gospel of Christ; and it was with feelings of deep sorrow that he heard with his own ears in the House of Lords the charge brought against the present Governor-General of India, that he had given a contribution to a Missionary Society. That was imputed to him as a crime, and as a grievous wrong to the religion of the country over which he was called to govern. Did it not seem that this was a retribution for their conduct towards that empire? If they had civilized, if they had christianized those who had now turned round upon them with such barbarous ferocity, they would not have been exposed to those calamities which have befallen them. They were guilty as a nation for not having boldly taught that religion to others which they professed themselves. Earnestly did he hope that the result of the war might lead to the adoption of a different policy by this country." The unworthy fear that our empire in the East would be endangered by our discouragement of and interference as a *Christian* Government with the superstitions of the people, is refuted by the fact that in those parts of India where missionary labours have been most active and most successful, there order and safety are enjoyed, and this rebellious outbreak, with its attendant horrors, are but little felt or feared.

It is an opinion, confirmed by the testimony of missionaries and others resident in India, and best acquainted with the feelings of the people, that this fearful outbreak of violence and insurrection is to be traced not to any real or imaginary wrongs done to India, but that it is mainly a *religious*, a *Mohammedan* movement, having for its object not only the overthrow of British dominion, but the expulsion and extirpation of all Christians and Christianity from India. The violence, the unparalleled cruelties on Christians, is but acting out the principles inculcated in the Shasters of the Hindoos, and especially in the Koran of the Mohammedans. And is it not humiliating and astounding that in the schools established for native instruction by the Indian Government, that the Shaster and the Koran should be received in those schools as books of instruction while, at the same time, the holy Scriptures are ignored and proscribed? An Indian officer in the Madras Presidency thus writes: "You will have seen that we are now passing through what is, without doubt, the greatest peril to which our Indian Empire has ever been exposed. I do not feel at all doubtful as to its ultimate issue, because I feel persuaded that our mission in India has not yet been fulfilled; and because the present fierce outbreak, whatever may be its real cause, has been distinctly put by the mutineers themselves, Mohammedans as well as Hindoos, *upon the ground of religion.* It has the character, consequently, of an open contest for Satan against Christ, and 'He shall have them in derision.'"

What, then, is the duty of the Home and of the Indian Government, on the putting down of the present rebellion in India, with a view to the re-settlement and re-construction of the government of our Eastern Empire? It is required that we act towards India *as a decidedly Christian Power*. That no direct encouragement be given to idolatry, no favouritism or preference be shown to idolaters, or to *castes*, the existence, tolerance, and influence of which are the source of so many social evils in India, and the cause, in a great measure, of the present calamities. In the administration of righteous and equal laws for all, in our civil and military employments, *caste* must not be recognized as a qualification or a ground of preference, or conversion to Christianity a disadvantage or disqualification. In the Indian schools patronized by the Government, the Holy Scriptures must be admitted and used for instruction. "Mere *secular* education without the Word of God," as a missionary justly remarks, "is training up a race of infidels, and not the right way to make loyal subjects for Queen Victoria—to say nothing of aught else." Though it is not the duty of a Christian Government to attempt by *coercion* the putting down of the false religions and debasing superstitions of India, it is clearly its duty as a Christian Power that full means of Christian instruction be provided for the natives, that every part of the country be fully and freely opened to Christian missionaries, and that all protection and encouragement be given to them. The Church of God must awake and arise to a deeper sense of the duty of doing more, and of making greater efforts and sacrifices for the christianization of India than she has ever yet done.

Though at present dark clouds brood over our Eastern Empire, yet the Christian believer in the revealed purposes and promises of God—not doubting for a moment that what is now happening "will turn out rather unto the furtherance of the Gospel"—will look forward with faith and hope to brighter and better days for that dark land. The Gospel, which has triumphed over the formidable superstitions of olden times, has lost nothing of its heavenly power. It has already achieved glorious triumphs in India. The seed of the Word of God has been widely sown there, and will yield a glorious harvest. The light of the Gospel which has broken upon those dark places of the earth heralds a coming glorious day. What though as yet it resembles the dim twilight of the morning breaking gently on the long deathlike slumbers of the millions there, it is surely leading on to the full splendours of the day when God will "destroy the covering cast over all people, and the vail that is spread over all nations." India shall one day cast away her idols and her superstitions, and become "the Kingdom of our God and his *Christ*,"—"As surely as I live, saith the Lord, the whole earth shall be filled with his glory."

"Come forth out of Thy royal chambers, O Prince of all the kings of the earth; put on the visible robes of Thy imperial majesty, take up that unlimited sceptre which Thy Almighty Father hath bequeathed Thee; for now the voice of the Bride calls Thee, and all creatures sigh to be renewed."—MILTON.

Macintosh, Printer, Great New-street, London.

BY THE SAME AUTHOR.

The Mutual Recognition of Glorified Saints. Sixth Edition. 3*s.* 6*d.*

Reasons for Attachment and Conformity to the Church of England. Third Edition. 18mo., cloth, 2*s.* 6*d.*

The Church of England a Faithful Witness against the Errors and Corruptions of the Church of Rome. 8vo., boards, 12*s.*

Passion Week: a Practical and Devotional Exposition of the Gospels and Epistles appointed for that season, composed for the Closet and the Family. 12mo., boards, 4*s.*

The Time of Affliction. 12mo., 2*s.* 6*d.*

Practical and Devotional Meditations on the Lord's Supper. 32mo., cloth, 2*s.* 6*d.*

Christian Duties for the Closet. 12mo., 2*s.* 6*d.*

Heavenly Things. 12mo., 3*s.* 6*d.*

&c., &c., &c.

BY MRS. MEEK.

Thoughts on the Responsibility of Man; with a view to the Amelioration of Society. Addressed to the Higher and Middle Classes. Foolscap, cloth, 3*s.* 6*d.*

A Biographical Sketch of Sir Henry Havelock, K.C.B. Compiled from Original Papers. By the Rev. WILLIAM BROCK. Crown 8vo., 3*s*. 6*d*. cloth.

Memorials of Captain Hedley Vicars, 97th Regiment. By the Author of "The Victory Won." Small crown 8vo., 3*s*. 6*d*. cloth.

A Memoir of Adelaide L. Newton. By the Rev. JOHN BAILLIE, Author of "Memoirs of W. H. Hewitson." Small crown 8vo., 5*s*. cloth.

A Memoir of Lady Colquhoun of Luss. By the Rev. JAMES HAMILTON, D.D. 7*s*. 6*d*. cloth.

A Memoir of Richard Williams, Surgeon, Catechist in the Mission to Patagonia, Tierra del Fuego. By JAMES HAMILTON, D.D. With Portrait. Crown 8vo., 3*s*. 6*d*. cloth.

Memorials of the late Dr. Townley. By the Rev. SAMUEL MARTIN, Westminster. Crown 8vo., 5*s*. cloth.

A Memoir and Remains of the Rev. J. Harington Evans, M.A. By the Rev. J. JOYCE EVANS, M.A. Crown 8vo., 7*s*. 6*d*. cloth.

Memoir of the late Rev. W. H. Hewitson, Dirleton. By the Rev. JOHN BAILLIE. Crown 8vo., 5*s*. cloth, and 1*s*. 6*d*. sewed.

A Memoir of the late Capt. Allen Gardiner, R.N. By the Rev. J. W. MARSH, Vicar of Bleasby, Notts. Crown 8vo., 5*s*. cloth.

A Stranger Here. A Memorial of One of whom to live was Christ, and to die was gain. By the Rev. HORATIUS BONAR, D.D. Fcap., 5*s*. cloth.

A Memoir of the Life and Labours of the Rev. A. Judson, D.D., Missionary to Burmah. By FRANCIS WAYLAND, D.D. 2 vols. 8vo., 12*s*. cloth.

A Memoir of the Rev. J. J. Weitbrecht, late Missionary of the Church Missionary Society in Bengal. Compiled by his Widow from his Journals and Letters. With a Preface by the Rev. H. VENN, M.A. Second Edition. Crown 8vo., 7*s*. 6*d*.